10.95   3-14-02   Southeast   T

M000211385

The Sayings of Benjamin Franklin

Sayings of Jane Austen
Sayings of Lord Byron
Sayings of Winston Churchill
Sayings of Charles Dickens
Sayings of Disraeli
Sayings of F. Scott Fitzgerald
Sayings of Benjamin Franklin
Sayings of Dr Johnson
Sayings of James Joyce
Sayings of John Keats
Sayings of Rudyard Kipling
Sayings of D.H. Lawrence
Sayings of Somerset Maugham
Sayings of Nietzsche
Sayings of George Orwell
Sayings of Dorothy Parker
Sayings of Ezra Pound
Sayings of Sir Walter Scott
Sayings of Shakespeare
Sayings of Bernard Shaw
Sayings of Sydney Smith
Sayings of R.L. Stevenson
Sayings of Jonathan Swift
Sayings of Leo Tolstoy
Sayings of Anthony Trollope
Sayings of Mark Twain
Sayings of Oscar Wilde
Sayings of W.B. Yeats
Sayings of the Bible
Sayings of the Buddha
Sayings of Jesus
Sayings of Moses
Sayings of Muhammad

The Sayings of

BENJAMIN
FRANKLIN

edited by
E. Wright

DUCKWORTH

First published in 1995 by
Gerald Duckworth & Co. Ltd.
The Old Piano Factory
48 Hoxton Square, London N1 6PB
Tel: 0171 729 5986
Fax: 0171 729 0015

A catalogue record for this book is available
from the British Library

ISBN 0 7156 2620 5

Typeset by Ray Davies
Printed in Great Britain by
Redwood Books Ltd, Trowbridge

Contents

Our new Constitution is now established, and
has an appearance that promises permanency
but in this world nothing can be said to be
certain, except death and taxes.

13 November 1789, *Writings* X 69

Introduction

Benjamin Franklin's life is probably the best known in American history. The tenth and youngest son and fifteenth child in a family of seventeen children, he was born in colonial Boston in 1706. His father was a tallow-chandler and soap-boiler who had left Northamptonshire in England twenty-three years before.

With less than two years' formal schooling behind him, and with the knowledge of the printing trade that he acquired in the course of an apprenticeship to one of his brothers, Benjamin Franklin was not trained as a scholar. But he read voraciously: Addison's *Spectator*, Bunyan's *Pilgrim's Progress*, Plutarch's *Lives*, Defoe's *Essay on Projects*, Cotton Mather's *Essays To Do Good*. 'I do not remember when I could not read.' 'All the little Money that came into my hands was ever laid out in books.' Bunyan's idiom and style, the characters and their abodes left a permanent imprint: Mr Worldly Wiseman and Mr Legality, Mr Obstinate and Mr Pliable, the Delectable Mountains and Vanity Fair have echoes in Franklin's pages.

Benjamin Franklin ran away from home – first to New York and then to Philadelphia, where, after an eighteen-month spell in London, he finally launched himself as a printer and journalist, a wordsman and an inventor. He then married, and embarked upon a hectic round of civic activities, becoming an Assembly-man and politician, interesting himself in the nature of electricity, and founding a hospital, a college, a library, a fire-company and a fire insurance system. One can understand the fashionable Philadelphia view that Franklin was born (or perhaps one should say 'born again') in Philadelphia at the age of seventeen; for from that age the city became his base for a host of enterprises.

From 1733 to 1758 Franklin also published *Poor Richard's Almanack*. This was a familiar format – when Franklin's first appeared, there were already six almanacks being printed in Philadelphia. In *Poor Richard* Franklin printed common-sense observations and wise saws, culled mainly from Rabelais, Swift and Sterne – and he did not pretend to any originality: 'gleanings', he called them, 'of all ages and nations'. 'Why should I give my readers bad lines of my own, when good ones of other people's are so plenty?' He made the *Almanack* not only the formula for his own financial success but the first great syndicated column in American journalism. He served up a rich fare: maxims, epigrams and proverbs, welcome as much for their familiarity as for their terseness; much commonplace moralising, much worldly shrewdness, not a little bawdiness – for 'squeamish stomachs cannot eat without pickles'.

If many of these proverbs were centuries old, Franklin gave them vigour, clarity and punch, transforming them in the process. The Scots proverb 'A listening damsel and a speaking castle shall never end with honour' became, in Franklin's version, 'Neither a fortress nor a maid will hold out long after they begin to parley.' The English proverb 'God restoreth health and the physician hath the thanks' was changed to 'God restoreth health and the physician takes the fee.' 'Fresh fish and newcome guests smell, but that they are three days old' became, recalling his father's view on visits from relations, 'Fish and guests stink after three days.'

Poor Richard has been regarded by many as the mentor of early American capitalism: as the high priest of thrift, savings banks, insurance. 'Keep thy shop,' said Poor Richard, 'and thy shop will keep thee.' His advice is certainly keyed to the two notes struck in his sayings: 'Work hard and count your pennies'; 'The sleeping fox catches no poultry'; 'Then plough deep, while sluggards sleep, and you shall have corn to sell and to keep'; 'Lost time is never found again'; 'He that hath a trade hath an estate, and he that hath a calling hath an office of profit and honour.'

The identification of Poor Richard with these principles was due to the collection of those sayings exhorting to industry and frugality into the preface to the 1757 *Almanack*, to be put in the mouth of Father Abraham, and then to be separately printed as *The Way to Wealth*. It became, as *Bonhomme Richard*, fashionable in France (with immeasurable consequences in 1776). It has gone through some 1,300 editions since it was first compiled.

Not that all Poor Richard's moralities were exhortations to business enterprise. Some were of a homelier and an earthier sort. 'Love your neighbour, but don't pull down your hedge'; 'When you are good to others, you are best to yourself '; 'Three may keep a secret if two of them are dead'; 'A single man is like the odd half of a pair of scissors'; 'He that takes a wife takes care'; 'Keep your eyes wide open before marriage, half shut afterwards'; 'You cannot pluck roses without fear of thorns, nor enjoy a fair wife without danger of horns'. Yet in nothing is Franklin more typical of his century and of his country than in his insistence that self-reliance and hard work are basic to liberty. A political creed was clear, but left, as always, implicit. He believed in free speech, free goods and free men. He opposed the efforts of all exploiters, whether merchants from England, Scots factors in America, land-owners or priests, to restrain man's natural freedoms. And freedom, he argued, paid.

When he moved to London in 1757, as agent for the Pennsylvania Assembly, he described his personal life as that of an Old England Man. He lodged in Craven Street, just off Charing Cross –

> For the Lawyers are just at the top of the street
> And the Barges are just at the bottom.
> Fly, honesty, fly to some safer retreat
> For there's craft in the river and craft in the street.

His landlady, the widow Mrs Margaret Stevenson, adopted him as a sort of foster-father, and his letters to her and her daugher Mary (Polly), who in the end was to be his housekeeper at Passy and to settle in Philadelphia, are delightful and affectionate. He installed an electric machine and carried out experiments in his ample suite of four furnished rooms at the top of the house – 'and everything about us pretty genteel'. He hoped that Polly would marry his son William, but whatever her feelings might have been, William, who had studied or at least been enrolled at the Middle Temple, had by August 1762 become engaged to Elizabeth Downes from the West Indies, thus breaking off his

earlier engagement to Elizabeth Graeme of
Philadelphia. William had also early in 1760
fathered – it seemed an hereditary trait – an
illegitimate son, William Temple Franklin.
Neither of these activities prevented his
becoming Governor of New Jersey, at the age
of 31; presumably his father was now a man
for government to cultivate.

There can be little doubt that Franklin liked
the London life, on the edge of public affairs
and acquainted with the great. He lived well:
a coach of his own and his two negro servants,
King and Peter, whom he and his son William
had taken with them – though King ran away
after a year. His critics back at base knew of
and resented his comfort. James Hamilton,
ex-Governor and now a member of council,
criticised the cost of his mission. 'Yet what is
this to Mr Franklin? Hath it not afforded him
a life of pleasure and an opportunity of
displaying his talents among the virtuosi of
various Kingdoms and nations?'

His eight Atlantic crossings were always
occasions for recording natural phenomena:
ocean temperatures, storms, currents, the
partial eclipse of the moon. London added its
own stimulus in 1726: he met Mandeville, the
author of the *Fable of the Bees* – 'a most face-
tious, entertaining companion' – and Dr
Pemberton, the Secretary of the Royal Society;
he hoped but failed to see Newton. On his

return, his newspaper begins to reflect the range of his interests: the weather and waterspouts, why salt dissolves in water, why the sea is sometimes luminous, cures of kidney stones and cancer, mortality rates in Philadelphia, and how many people could stand in an area of one hundred square yards. Even in the political crises after 1765 he can write at length on a scheme for a new alphabet, or his magic squares, or elephant tusks, or the sepulchres of Scythian Kings, or the ways of ants, or of pigeons, or of farmers. And he expressed himself only in part facetiously, when after the crossing in July 1757, from New York to Falmouth in the packet *General Wall* and just missing shipwreck off the Scillies, he wrote to Debby: 'The bell ringing for church, we went thither immediately, and with hearts full of gratitude, returned sincere thanks to God for the mercies we had received: were I a Roman Catholic, perhaps I should on this occasion vow to build a chapel to some saint; but as I am not, if I were to vow at all, it should be to build a lighthouse.'

Franklin as well as Poor Richard is his own creation. He made books, and he made and invented news – and his books and his news 'made' him. When he began his *Autobiography* in 1771, a tale dotted with moral precepts and much self-revelation, it was done with a twinkle and a sunny humour – and yet always with a touch of reserve.

There is evident recognition on his part that he is now a public figure, a symbol not only in Paris but in America too; and he writes with coolness and irony, however earnest the exhortations. He was, moreover, remote from his own books and records, even from the first part of his story which, along with his papers, he had left for safe-keeping – or so he thought – with his friend and former political colleague, Joseph Galloway, at his home in Trevose outside Philadelphia. In 1776 when Lord Howe's forces occupied Philadelphia, however, Galloway had become a Loyalist and had then moved to London: Grace Galloway was forcibly evicted from their Philadelphia townhouse at 6th and Market Street by a group led by the artist-patriot Charles Willson Peale, and the house later became the residence of President Washington. As a result, the 'Franklin Papers' – so the news reached Passy – had been scattered to the winds.

Benjamin Franklin lived a long life, in five distinct places, Boston, Philadelphia, London, Scotland and Passy, now the sixteenth sector of Paris, but then a village, and he saw more of his world than most of his contemporaries. He would have been content to settle and to die in any one of them, for this was the the most adaptable of men. He lived through stormy and changing times, and through

them went on 'swimmingly'. Intellectually, he
was born a Calvinist and ended a deist; politi-
cally, the Old England Man who was the
servant of the Empire in many jobs, and
would have welcomed more, ended as a
republican; the slave-owner and advertiser of
slave auctions became strongly anti-slavery;
the racist and WASP of 1751 became the
Francophile of 1782-3; a poor and ill-educated
boy in a family of 17, he raised himself by his
skill with and the selling of words, to retire
wealthy at 42, in order to be what he had
always wanted to be: a philosopher. He
sought to give shape and meaning to his
immense range of interests but became in fact
a man of many causes: republicanism, federal-
ism, unicameralism were only some of them,
and not the most important. What was central
to Franklin, and the theme to which he stayed
constant, was the quest for, and the application of, knowledge. This could easily be –
indeed was best – studied in many different
locales, for it depended on the pooling of
many minds. Knowledge, and its application
to the real world, was the central thread; it
should, wherever possible, be put to use.
Franklin was as skilful with his hands as he
was with his pen. Thus he devised bifocals
and a flexible catheter – and stoves and
lightning rods, timepieces and balloons,
colleges and hospitals, fire-protection and

fire-insurance. He wanted to go on living just to meet the fascination of the changes that were to come. He wanted particularly to see the changes in the New World, whose independence he had helped to secure by his negotiations in Paris in 1782.

Nor was he averse from playing tricks, as he did in the park at Wycombe in 1772, as a guest at Lord Shelburne's country house where his fellow guests included David Garrick the actor and Col. Isaac Barré. Seeing a stream being whipped by the wind he claimed the ability to quiet the waters. He walked 200 paces from his companions and made some magic passes over the water with his bamboo cane. The water sank and the stream became as smooth as a mirror. He then revealed that the artifice was in his scientific knowledge: concealed in a hollow joint in the cane was enough oil to do the trick. In country-house circles it was helpful to be Franklin the Magician.

Moreover, both among his puritan and his romantic and 'life-force' critics, to whom he seemed at best prudent and at worst hypocritical, even his humour was distasteful. He learnt early that a smile and a twinkle in the prose made it readable, and humour became one of his weapons. At times it is spicy and colloquial, at others Biblical and rhetorical; it could be anecdotal at one moment and satirical the next – and it was always honed to sparkle and to pierce. It may well have been as carefully cultivated as much else in his character. It responded clearly to his leather-apron vigour. He was not trusted to draft the Declaration of Independence, it has often been said, lest he put a joke in it. Balzac summarised his career succinctly: Franklin, he said, invented the lightning rod, the hoax and the Republic.

Franklin died in Philadelphia 17 April 1790 after a long illness, aged eighty-four. He was buried in Christ Church Burial Ground, attended by a crowd of some 20,000, the largest ever to assemble in Philadelphia. The tomb has his own simple wording, as his will directed: 'Benjamin and Deborah Franklin: 1790.'

But the epitaph by which he is remembered he had written himself, with wry humour, sixty-two years before:

The body of
B. Franklin, Printer
(Like the Cover of an Old Book
Its Contents Torn Out
And Stript of its Lettering and Gilding)
Lies Here, Food for Worms.
But the Work shall not be Lost;
For it will (as he Believ'd) Appear once More
In a New and More Elegant Edition
Revised and Corrected
By the Author.

Sources

In preparing this volume, I have relied in large measure upon *The Papers of Benjamin Franklin*, 31 volumes thus far, which bring the story to 1782 (L.W. Labaree, W.B. Willcox, Claude-Anne Lopez, Barbara Oberg et al. (eds), Yale University Press, since 1959); upon A.H. Smyth's edition of *The Writings of Benjamin Franklin* (Macmillan, 1905-07, 10 vols); upon the Yale edition of *The Autobiography* (L.W. Labaree, Ralph L. Ketcham, Helen C. Boatfield, Helene H. Fineman (eds), Yale University Press, 1964), its impressive scholarly apparatus and biographical notes; and upon the resources of the American Philosophical Society in Philadelphia.

See also Carl Van Doren, *Benjamin Franklin* (Viking Press, 1938); Alfred Owen Aldridge, *Franklin and His French Contemporaries* (New York University Press, 1957); J.A. Leo Lemay, *Benjamin Franklin, Writings* (Library of America, 1987), Claude-Anne Lopez, *Mon Cher Papa: Franklin and the Ladies of Paris* (Yale University Press, 1966); Esmond Wright, *Franklin of Philadelphia* (Harvard University Press, 1986).

A certain amount of editing of the text has been undertaken in the interests of consistency, but Franklin's use of italics and his sometimes idiosyncratic spelling have been retained. Omissions within the text are marked by ellipses (...).

Abbreviations

Autobiography	*The Autobiography* (Yale edition, 1964)
P.R.A.	*Poor Richard's Almanack* (Yale Papers)
P.G.	*Pennsylvania Gazette*
Bag.	*The Bagatelles,* written and printed at Passy
Writings	Smyth A.H. (ed.), *Writings of Benjamin Franklin* (Macmillan, 1905) 10 vols.
Papers	*The Papers of Benjamin Franklin* (Yale University associated with American Philosophical Society) 31 vols. thus far.

National Wealth & Taxation

There seem to be but three Ways for a Nation to acquire Wealth. The first is by *War* as the Romans did in plundering their conquered Neighbours. This is *Robbery*. The second by *Commerce* which is generally *Cheating*. The third by *Agriculture* the only *honest Way*; wherein Man receives a real Increase of the Seed thrown into the Ground, in a kind of continual Miracle wrought by the Hand of God in his Favour, as a Reward for his innocent life, and virtuous Industry. B.F.

Positions to be examin'd, 4 April 1769,
Papers XVI 109

The number of purely white people in the world is proportionably very small. All *Africa* is black or tawny; *Asia* chiefly tawny; *America* (exclusive of the newcomers) wholly so. And in *Europe*, the *Spaniards*, ... Why increase the sons of Africa by planting them in *America*, where we have so fair an opportunity, by excluding all blacks and tawnys, of increasing the lovely white and red? But perhaps I am partial to the complexion of my country, for such kind of partiality is natural to mankind.

Observations concerning the Increase of Mankind,
Penn. 1751, *Papers* IV 228-9

[On 4 February 1748, Franklin recorded the birth of] Louis the 15th, present King of France, called his most christian majesty. He bids fair to be as great a mischief-maker as his grandfather; or in the language of poets and orators, a Hero. There are three great destroyers of mankind, Plague, Famine, and Hero. Plagues and Famine destroy your persons only, and leave your goods to your Heirs; but Hero when he comes, takes life and goods together; his business and glory it is to destroy men and the Works of man.

P.R.A., February 1748

Kings and Bears often worry their Keepers.

P.R.A., January 1739

If you ride a Horse, sit close and tight,
If you ride a Man, sit easy and light.

P.R.A., April 1734

We are taxed twice as much by our Idleness, three times as much by our Pride, and four times as much by our Folly.

To Robert Morris, Passy, 25 December 1785,
Writings IX 138

Idleness and Pride tax with a heavier hand than Kings and Parliaments.

To Charles Thomson, London, 11 July 1765,
Writings IV 389

So vast is the territory of *North America,* that it will require many ages to settle it fully; and, until it is fully settled, labour will never be cheap here, where no man continues long a labourer for others, but gets a plantation of his own, no man continues long a journeyman to trade, but goes among those new settlers, and sets up for himself etc.

Observations concerning the Increase of Mankind,
Penn. 1751, *Papers* IV 228

Great beauty, great strength, and great riches are really and truly of no great use; a right heart exceeds all.

P.R.A., December 1739

Public Office

The first mistake in public business is the
going into it.

Preface to *P.R.A.*, 1758

To serve the Publick faithfully, and at the
same time please it entirely, is impracticable.

P.R.A., October 1758

In a discreet man's mouth, a publick thing is
private.

P.R.A., March 1736

The Horse thinks one thing, He that saddles
him another.

P.R.A., April 1754

You may give a man an office, but you cannot
give him discretion.

P.R.A., August 1754

The greatest monarch on the proudest throne
Is oblig'd to sit upon his own arse.

P.R.A., January 1737

Mad Kings and mad Bulls are not to be held
by treaties and packthread.

P.R.A., October 1746

Glass, China and Reputation are easily crack'd
And Never well mended.

P.R.A., December 1750

There's a Time to wink as well as to see.

P.R.A., March 1747

Here comes the Orator! with his flood of
words, and his drop of reason.

P.R.A., October 1735

If you would reap Praise you must sow the
  Seeds,
Gentle words and useful Deeds.

P.R.A., May 1753

In rivers and bad Governments,
The lightest things swim at the top.

P.R.A., March 1754

He that cannot obey, cannot command.

P.R.A., August 1734

The Old England Man

The whole town is one great smoky house and every street a chimney, the air full of floating sea coal soot and you never get a sweet breath of what is pure without riding some miles for it into the country.

To his wife Deborah after reaching London,
17 February 1758, *Papers* VII 380

Of all the enviable things England has, I envy it most its People. Why should that petty Island, which compar'd to America, is but like a stepping-stone in a Brook, scarce enough of it above Water to keep one's Shoes dry; why, I say, should that little Island enjoy in almost every Neighbourhood, more sensible, virtuous, and elegant Minds, than we can collect in ranging 100 Leagues of our vast Forests? But 'tis said the Arts delight to travel Westward.

To Polly Stevenson, 25 March 1763,
Writings IV 194

... the foundations of the future Grandeur and Stability of the British Empire lie in America, and tho', like other Foundations, they are low and little seen, they are nevertheless broad and strong enough to support the greatest Political Structure Human Wisdom ever yet erected.

To Lord Kames, 3 January 1760, *Papers* XI 7

America, an immense territory, favoured by nature with all advantages of climate, soil, great navigable rivers, and lakes etc., must become a great country, populous and mighty; and will, in a less time than is generally conceived, be able to shake of any shackles that may be imposed on her, and perhaps place them on the imposers. In the mean time, every act of oppression will sour their tempers, lessen greatly, if not annihilate the profits of your commerce with them, and hasten their final revolt; for the seeds of liberty are universally found there, and nothing can eradicate them.

To Lord Kames, 26 February 1767,
Papers XIV 68-70

Long did I endeavour, with unfeigned and unwearied zeal, to preserve from breaking that fine and noble china vase, the British Empire for I knew that, being once broken, the separate parts could not retain even their shares of the strength or value that existed in the whole, and that a perfect reunion of those parts could scarce ever be hoped for. Your lordship may possibly remember the tears of joy that wet my cheek when, at your good sister's in London, you once gave me expectations that a reconciliation might soon take place. I had the misfortune to find those expectations disappointed, and to be treated as the cause of the mischief I was labouring to prevent.

I consider this war against us, therefore, as unjust and unwise; and I am persuaded that cool, dispassionate posterity will condemn to infamy those who advised it; and that even success will not save from some degree of dishonour those who voluntarily engaged to conduct it. I know your great motive in coming hither was the hope of being instrumental in a reconciliation; and I believe, when you find *that* to be impossible on any terms given you to propose, you will relinquish so odious a command and return to a more honourable private station.

To Admiral Lord Howe, off Staten Island,
20 July 1776, *Papers* XXII 520

The Virtuous Life

Virtue and Happiness are Mother and
Daughter.

P.R.A., May 1746

There are three things extremely hard, steel, a
diamond, and to know one's self.

P.R.A., January 1750

There's none deceived but he that trusts.

P.R.A., October 1736

Better is a little with content than much with
Contention.

P.R.A., October 1747

Sin is not hurtful because it is forbidden. But it
is forbidden because it is hurtful.

P.R.A., December 1739

He that best understands the World, least
likes it.   *P.R.A.*, June 1753

Despair ruins some, Presumption many.

P.R.A., July 1747

We may give Advice, we cannot give Conduct.

P.R.A., February 1751

Keep thou from the Opportunity, and God will keep thee from the Sin.

P.R.A., August 1744

Early to bed, early to rise, Makes a Man Healthy, Wealthy and Wise.

P.R.A., October 1735

Prosperity discovers Vice, Adversity Virtue.

P.R.A., January 1751

Tim was so learned that he could name a Horse in nine languages, but bought a cow to ride on.

P.R.A., November 1750

Content makes poor men rich, Discontent rich men poor.

P.R.A., April 1749

I have never seen the Philosopher's Stone that turns lead into Gold; but I have known the pursuit of it turn a Man's Gold into Lead.

P.R.A., September 1738

Each year one vicious habit rooted out, In time might make the Worst Man good throughout.

P.R.A., November 1738

He that falls in love with Himself, will have no Rivals.

P.R.A., May 1738

Proclaim not all thou knowest, all thou owest,
all thou hast, nor all thou canst.

P.R.A., 1739

Thou hadst better eat salt with the
philosophers of Greece than sugar with the
courtiers of Italy.

P.R.A., September 1740

Tho' Modesty is a Virtue,
Bashfulness is a Vice.

P.R.A., September 1750

To lead a virtuous Life, my Friends,
  And get to Heaven in Season
You've just so much more Need of Faith
  As you have less of Reason.

P.R.A., February 1748

Against diseases here, the strongest Fence
Is the defensive Virtue, Abstinence.

P.R.A., October 1742

Would you live with Ease,
Do what you ought, not what you please.

P.R.A., January 1734

There is no man so bad but he secretly
respects the good.

P.R.A., March 1747

Pardoning the bad is injuring the Good.

P.R.A., November 1748

Neither trust, nor contend, nor lay wagers,
   nor lend;
And you'll have peace to your life's end.
P.R.A., May 1749

The end of Passion is the beginning of
Repentance.
P.R.A., February 1749

The honest Man takes Pains, and then enjoys
Pleasures; the Knave takes Pleasure, and then
suffers Pains.
P.R.A., June 1755

Frugality & Industry

What maintains one Vice would bring up two
children.
P.R.A., September 1747

Many Estates are spent on the Getting
Since Women for Tea forsook Spinning and
Knitting
And Men for Punch forsook Hewing and
Splitting.
P.R.A., Preface 1758

Nothing but money is sweeter than honey.
P.R.A., June 1735

No man e'er was glorious
Who was not laborious.
P.R.A., March 1734

Cut the wings of your hens and hopes, lest
they lead you a weary dance after them.
P.R.A., February 1754

He does not possess wealth; it possesses him.
P.R.A., October 1734

Poverty wants some things, luxury many
things, avarice all things.
P.R.A., July 1735

Laziness travels so slowly that Poverty soon overtakes him.

P.R.A., September 1756

Up, sluggards, and waste no life; in the grave will be sleeping enough.

P.R.A., September 1741

He that riseth late must trot all day; and we shall scarce overtake his business at night.

P.R.A., August 1742

If you would know the value of Money, go and borrow some.

P.R.A., April 1754

Wealth is not his that has it, but his that enjoys it.

P.R.A., March 1736

When the well's dry, we know the worth of water.

P.R.A., January 1746

Three removes is as bad as a fire.

P.R.A., Preface 1758

Great Talkers, Little Doers.

P.R.A., February 1733

Diligence is the Mother of Good Luck.

P.R.A., February 1736

Lying rides upon debt's back.

P.R.A., July 1741

If you'd be wealthy, think of saving, more than of getting. The Indies have not made Spain rich, because her Outgoes equal her Incomes.

P.R.A., October 1743

He that hath a Trade, hath an Office of Profit and Honour.

P.R.A., March 1756

Faith

Think of three Things, whence you came, where you are going, and to whom you must account.
P.R.A., May 1755

Talking against Religion is unchaining a Tyger; The Beast let loose may worry his Deliverer.
P.R.A., September 1759

What is serving God?
'Tis doing good to Man.
P.R.A., September 1747

None preaches better than the ant, and she says nothing.
P.R.A., July 1736

Serving God is doing Good to Man, but Praying is thought an easier Service, and therefore more generally chosen.
P.R.A., November 1753

A good example is the best sermon.
P.R.A., June 1747

In the affairs of this world, men are saved not by faith but by the want of it.
P.R.A., June 1754

Many have quarrelled about religion that
never practis'd it.   *P.R.A.*, June 1753

The Bells call others to Church
But itself never minds the Sermon.
                                       P.R.A., February 1754

Men differ daily, about things which are
subject to sense; is it likely that they should
agree about things invisible.   *P.R.A.*, January 1743

Certainlie these things agree,
The Priest, the Lawyer and Death all three:
Death takes both the weak and the strong,
The Lawyer takes from both right and wrong,
And the Priest from living and dead has his
    Fee.   *P.R.A.*, July 1737

Go constantly to church, whoever preaches.
The act of devotion to the *Common Prayer Book*
is your principal business there, and if
properly attended to, will do more toward
mending the heart than sermons generally
can do. For they were composed by men of
much greater piety and wisdom than our
common composers of sermons can pretend
to be; and therefore I wish you would never
miss the prayer days; yet I do not mean you
should despise sermons, even of the preachers
you dislike, for the discourse is often much
better than the man, as sweet and clear waters
come through very dirty earth.
            To Sarah Franklin, 8 November 1764, *Papers* XI 449

I have always set a greater Value on the Character of a Doer of Good, than on any other kind of Reputation.

To Samuel Mather, 12 May 1784, *Writings* IX 208

Many a long dispute among Divines may be thus abridg'd:
It is so, It is not so, It is so, It is not so.

P.R.A., November 1743

Marriage

He that takes a Wife, takes Care.

P.R.A., 1736

If Jack's in love, he's no judge of Jill's beauty.

P.R.A., October 1748

A single man … is an incomplete animal. He resembles the odd half of a pair of scissors.

Advice to a Young Man on the Choice of a Mistress,
25 June 1745, Papers III 127-31

An undutiful Daughter, will prove an unmanageable wife.

P.R.A., August 1752

Old Boys have their Playthings as well as Young Ones; the Difference is only in the Price.

P.R.A., August 1752

Where there's marriage without love there will be love without marriage.

P.R.A., May 1734

He that hath not got a Wife, is not yet a compleat Man.

P.R.A., February 1744

An old young man will be a young old man.

P.R.A., November 1735

You cannot pluck roses without fear of thorns,
Nor enjoy a fair wife without danger of horns.

P.R.A., January 1734

Keep your eyes wide open before marriage,
half shut afterwards.

P.R.A., June 1738

She that will eat her breakfast in bed,
And spend the morn in dressing of her head.
And sit at dinner like a maiden bride,
And talk of nothing all day but of pride;
God in his mercy may do much to save her,
But what a case is he in that shall have her.

P.R.A., December 1733

Good wives and good plantations are made
by good husbands.

P.R.A., July 1736

When a man and woman die, as poets sung,
His heart's the last part moves, – her last, the
tongue.

P.R.A., September 1739

A little house well filled, a little field well
tilled, and a little wife well willed, are great
riches.

P.R.A., February 1735

A House without women and firelight, is like
a body without soul or sprite.

P.R.A., January 1733

Ne'er take a Wife 'till thou hast a House (and
a fire) to put her in.

P.R.A., February 1733

There are no ugly loves, nor handsome
prisons.

P.R.A., May 1737

Marry your Son when you will, but your
daughter when you can.

P.R.A., November 1734

If you would be loved, love and be loveable.

P.R.A., February 1755

A ship under sail and a big-bellied woman are
the handsomest two things that can be seen
common.

P.R.A., June 1735

My sickly Spouse, with many a Sigh
Once told me, – Dicky I shall die:
I griev'd, but recollected strait,
'Twas bootless to contend with Fate:
So Resignation to Heav'n's Will
Prepared me for succeeding Ill;
'Twas well it did; for, on my Life,
'Twas Heav'n's Will to spare my Wife.

P.R.A., January 1740

I am about Courting a Girl I have had but
little Acquaintance with; how shall I come to a
Knowledge of our Fawlts? and whether she
has the Virtues I imagine she has?
Answ. Commend her among her Female
Acquaintances.

P.G., 12 March 1732

Three things are men most liable to be cheated
in: A Horse, A Wig, A Wife.

P.R.A., October 1736

You can bear your own faults,
Why not a fault in your wife?

P.R.A., October 1750

Food & Drink

Squeamish stomachs cannot eat without pickles, which, 'tis true, are good for nothing else, but they provoke an appetite.

P.R.A., March 1734

What one relishes, nourishes.

P.R.A., March 1734

Never spare the parson's wine nor the baker's pudding.

P.R.A., January 1733

Men and melons are hard to know.

P.R.A., September 1733

He that drinks fast, pays slow.

P.R.A., August 1733

Take counsel in wine, but resolve afterwards in water.

P.R.A., August 1733

Hunger never saw bad bread.

P.R.A., February 1733

Beware of Meat twice boil'd, and an old foe reconciled.

P.R.A., April 1733

Fools make feasts and wise men eat 'em.
P.R.A., May 1733

Eat to live, and not live to eat.
P.R.A., May 1733

The poor have little, beggars none,
The rich too much, Enough not one.
P.R.A., May 1733

Keep your mouth wet, feet dry.
P.R.A., October 1733

To lengthen thy Life, lessen thy Meals.
P.R.A., June 1733

Hot things, sharp things, sweet things, cold
    things
All rot the teeth, and make them look like old
    things.
P.R.A., February 1734

Dine with little, sup with less,
Do better still – sleep supperless.
P.R.A., March 1744

It argues some shame in the drunkards
themselves that they have invented
numberless words and phrases to cover their
folly, whose proper significations are
harmless or have no signification at all. They
are seldom known to be drunk, though they

are very often boozey, cogey, tipsey, fox'd, merry, mellow, fuddled, groatable, confoundedly cut, see two moons; are among the Philistines, in a very good humor, see the sun, or, the sun has shone upon them; they clip the King's English, are almost froze, feverish, in their altitudes, pretty well enter'd etc.

Silence Dogood's Essay No. 12,
10 September 1722

A full Belly makes a dull Brain.
Poor Richard Improved, 1758

He that drinks his Cyder alone
Let him catch his Horse alone.
P.R.A., January 1744

A Wolf eats Sheep but now and then
Ten Thousand are devour'd by Men.
P.R.A., March 1740

He that spills the Rum, loses that only;
He that drinks it, often loses both that and himself.

P.R.A., July 1750

If it were not for the Belly, the Back might wear Gold.

P.R.A., February 1750

Tradesmen, Doctors & Lawyers

In order to secure my credit and character as a
tradesman, I took care not only to be in *reality*
industrious and frugal, but to avoid all
appearances of the contrary. I dressed plain and
was seen at no place of idle diversion. I never
went out a fishing or shooting; a book, indeed,
sometimes debauched me from my work, but
that was seldom, snug and gave no scandal ...
Thus being esteemed an industrious, thriving
young man, and paying duly for what I
bought ... I went on swimmingly.
Autobiography 125

Keep thy shop, and thy shop will keep thee.
P.R.A., June 1735

Great Estates may venture more,
Little Boats must keep near shore.
P.R.A., October 1751

He that hath a Trade, hath an Estate.
P.R.A., January 1742

There's more old drunkards than old doctors.
P.R.A., April 1736

God heals and the doctor takes the fee.
P.R.A., November 1736

Don't go to the doctor with every distemper, nor to the lawyer with every quarrel, nor to the pot for every thirst.
P.R.A., November 1737

He's the best physician that knows the worthlessness of the most medicines.
P.R.A., September 1733

He's a Fool that makes his Doctor his Heir.
P.R.A., February 1733

Be not sick too late, nor well too soon.
P.R.A., May 1734

Beware of the young Doctor and the old Barber.
P.R.A., May 1733

A countryman between two lawyers is like a fish between two cats.
P.R.A., February 1737

Lawyers, preachers and tomtit's eggs, there are more of them hatched than come to perfection.
P.R.A., May 1734

Visitors

He that lies down with dogs shall rise up with fleas.

P.R.A., July 1733

Visits should be short like a winter's day
Lest you're too troublesome, hasten away.

P.R.A., January 1733

After 3 days men grow weary, of a wench, a guest and weather rainy.

P.R.A., June 1733

Visit your aunt, but not every day; and call at your brother's, but not every night.

P.R.A., March 1742

If you'd lose a troublesome visitor, lend him money.

P.R.A., March 1744

The busy man has few idle Visitors: to the boiling pot the flies come not.

P.R.A., March 1752

Friendship increases by visiting Friends, but by visiting seldom.

P.R.A., June 1751

Love your neighbour, but don't pull down
your hedge.

P.R.A., April 1754

Liberality is not giving much, but giving
wisely.

P.R.A., May 1748

Friendship

Friends are the True Sceptres of Princes.

P.R.A., October 1754

A Father's a treasure, a Brother's a comfort, a Friend is both.

P.R.A., July 1747

Hear no ill of a Friend, nor speak any of an Enemy.

P.R.A., August 1739

Tis great confidence in a Friend to tell him *Your* Faults, greater to tell him *his*.

P.R.A., August 1751

Do good to thy friend to keep him, to thy enemy to gain him.

P.R.A., July 1734

The absent are never without fault, nor the present without excuse.

P.R.A., July 1736

There are three faithful friends,
An old wife, an old dog, and ready money.

P.R.A., January 1738

Education

Teach your child to hold his tongue,
He'll learn fast enough to speak.
P.R.A., July 1734

Let thy Child's first lesson be Obedience
And the second may be what thou wilt.
P.R.A., May 1739

Genius without education is like silver in the
mine.
P.R.A., August 1750

Read much, but not many books.
P.R.A., February 1738

Little Strokes fell Great Oaks.
P.R.A., August 1750

Reading makes a full Man,
    Meditation a profound Man,
        Discourse a clear Man.
P.R.A., October 1738

Want of Care does us more damage than want
of knowledge.
P.R.A., July 1746

If you wou'd not be forgotten,
  As soon as you are dead and rotten,
Either write things worth reading
  Or do things worth the writing.

P.R.A., May 1738

Printers indeed should be very careful how
they omit a Figure or a Letter; For by such
Means sometimes a terrible Alteration is made
in the Sense. I have heard, that once, in a new
Edition of the *Common Prayer*, the following
Sentence, *We shall all be changed in a Moment, in
the Twinkling of an Eye;* by the omission of a
single Letter, became, *We shall all be hanged in a
Moment,* &c. to the no small Surprize of the
first Congregation it was read to.

P.R.A., Preface 1750

Wisdom in the Mind is not, like Money in the
Purse, diminish'd by Communication to
others.

Preface to Galloway's Speech, 24 May 1764,
Writings IV 339

Learn of the Skilful; He that teaches himself,
hath a fool for his Master.

P.R.A., January 1741

What signifies knowing the Names, if you
know not the Natures of Things?

P.R.A., November 1750

Good & Bad Manners

Now I have a sheep and a cow, everybody
bids me good morrow.

P.R.A., June 1736

Look before or you'll find yourself behind.

P.R.A., January 1735

Approve not of him who commends all you
say.

P.R.A., January 1735

Write with the learned, pronounce with the
vulgar.

P.R.A., March 1738

Eat to please thyself, but dress to please others.

P.R.A., December 1738

Speak with contempt of none, from slave to
King,
The meanest Bee hath, and will use, a sting.

P.R.A., May 1743

Declaiming against Pride is not always a sign
of Humility.

P.R.A., September 1749

To err is human, to repent divine, to persist devilish.

P.R.A., November 1742

The wolf sheds his Coat once a Year, his Disposition never.

P.R.A., June 1755

Who is wise? He that learns from every One.
Who is powerful? He that governs his Passions.
Who is rich? He that is content.
Who is that? Nobody.

P.R.A., July 1755

If you have no Honey in your Pot, have some in your Mouth.

P.R.A., October 1753

A Pair of good Ears will drain dry an hundred Tongues.

P.R.A., October 1753

Nothing humbler than *Ambition*, when it is about to climb.

P.R.A., November 1753

Money and good Manners make the Gentleman.

P.R.A., March 1742

He is not well-bred, that cannot bear ill-breeding in others.

P.R.A., November 1748

Worldly Wisdom

Some are weather-wise, some otherwise.

P.R.A., February 1735

Three may keep a secret, if two of them are dead.

P.R.A., July 1735

Courage would fight, but discretion won't let him.

P.R.A., May 1747

There have been as great souls unknown to fame as any of the most famous.

P.R.A., November 1734

If your head is wax, don't walk in the sun.

P.R.A., July 1749

Many foxes grow gray, but few grow good.

P.R.A., March 1749

Would you persuade, speak of Interest, not Reason.

P.R.A., June 1734

Sal laughs at every thing you say.
Why? Because she has fine teeth.
P.R.A., November 1735

Why does the blind man's wife paint herself?
P.R.A., June 1736

When you speak to a man, look on his eyes;
When he speaks to thee, look on his mouth.
P.R.A., August 1740

Vanity backbites more than Malice.
P.R.A., March 1745

All would live long, but none would be old.
P.R.A., September 1749

Welcome, Mischief, if thou comest alone.
P.R.A., June 1749

Let all Men know thee, but no man know thee
   thoroughly:
Men freely ford that see the shallows.
P.R.A., July 1743

An ill wound, but not an ill Name, may be
healed. *P.R.A.*, July 1753

Philosophy as well as Foppery, often changes
Fashion.
P.R.A., January 1753

Patience in the Market, is worth pounds in a year.

P.R.A., September 1753

Many complain of their Memory, few of their Judgment.

P.R.A., August 1745

France

Various Impositions we suffer'd from
Boatmen, Porters etc on both Sides the Water.
I know not which are most rapacious, the
English or the French; but the latter have, with
their Knavery, the most Politeness.

To Polly Stevenson from Paris, 14 September
1767, Papers XIV 251

This is the civilest nation upon earth. Your
first acquaintances endeavour to find out
what you like and they will tell others. If 'tis
understood that you like mutton, dine where
you will you will find mutton. Somebody, it
seems, gave it out that I lov'd ladies; and then
everybody presented me their ladies (or the
ladies presented themselves) to be embraced –
that is to have their necks kissed. For as to
kissing of lips or cheeks, it is not the mode
here; the first is reckoned rude, and the other
may rub off the paint.

11 October 1779, Writings VII 393

The bearer of this who is going to America,
presses me to give him a Letter of
Recommendation, tho' I know nothing of him,
not even his name. This may seem
extraordinary, but I assure you it is not
uncommon here. Sometimes indeed one

unknown person brings me another equally unknown, to recommend him; and sometimes they recommend one another! As to this gentleman, I must refer you to himself for his character and merits, with which he is certainly better acquainted than I can possibly be. I recommend him however to those civilities which every stranger, of whom one knows no harm, has a right to, and I request you will do him all the good offices and show him all the favour that on further acquaintance you shall find him to deserve.

2 April 1777, *Papers* XXIII 550

Who's Who

Brillon, M. Hardancourt Brillon de Jouy (b. 1742), neighbour of Franklin in Passy.

Chaumont, Donatien-Leray Comte de (?-1803), Grand Master of the Woods and Forests of France. Honorary superintendent of the Hotel des Invalides. Owner of the Hotel de Valentinois, in which Franklin lived at Passy. Spent about two million francs, four-fifths of his entire fortune, in helping the American cause.

Collinson, Peter (1694-1763), London Quaker Merchant, FRS, one of the most important people in Franklin's life. A man of wide interests, he was a noted botanist who corresponded with Linnaeus and with colonial scientists, especially the botanist John Bartram. He was a great help to the Library Co. of Philadelphia and was responsible for the first publication, in 1751, of Franklin's *Experiments and Observations on Electricity*.

Franklin, Deborah Read Rogers (1708-74), married John Rogers, 1725, was deserted by him and became Franklin's plain, sensible wife and competent helper in business. Though she could not share his intellectual or social life, he cherished her and was usually indulgent, affectionate and generous. She did

not accompany him on his two English
missions, and she died, after a stroke, having
not seen him for ten years.

Franklin, James (1697-1783), Benjamin's
brother, learned the printer's trade in
England. Brought back a press, types and
supplies and started the *New England Courant*,
1721, a new and too lively kind of journalism
for Boston. In about 1726 he went to Newport,
where he published briefly the *Rhode Island
Gazette*, 1732-33, and became the public printer.

Franklin, Sarah (1743-1808), Franklin's
daughter, married Richard Bache (1737-1811),
b. Settle, Yorkshire, England, journalist.

Franklin, William (c. 1731-1813), son of
Benjamin. In 1750 his father described him as
'a tall proper Youth and much of a Beau'. A
close companion in many activities, he
succeeded the older man as a clerk of the
Assembly and post-master of Philadelphia,
had a brief military career, went to England
with his father in 1757, and entered the
Middle Temple to study law. He was
appointed royal governor of New Jersey,
1762. They took opposite sides in the events
leading to the Revolution; as a loyalist,
William was arrested and confined in
Connecticut, but was exchanged after two
years, remained with the British Army in New
York for nearly four years, and then went to
England. Though there was an attempted
reconciliation in 1785, Franklin almost wholly

excluded William in his last will: 'The part he
acted against me in the late War, which is of
public Notoriety, will account for my leaving
him no more of an Estate he endeavoured to
deprive me of.'

Helvetius, Claude-Adrian, Baron de (1715-71),
philosopher. Held office of *fermier general*,
which brought him an income of 300,000
francs per year. His book *De l'Esprit* was
banned by the parliament of Paris for its
freedom of opinion. Fled to England, thence to
Sans Souci (Berlin). Returned to France in 1771.

Helvetius, Mme de, b. Anne-Catherine de
Ligniville. Widow of the Baron. Lived at
Auteuil, near Passy. Hostess to and friend of
the *philosophes*.

Houdetot, Elizabeth-François, Sophie de la
Live de Bellegard, Comtesse de (1730-1815).
Franklin, Crevecoeur, Rousseau and
Saint-Lambert were her friends. Kept a
high-toned salon, unusually full of writers.
Wrote verse. Owned a great estate in Sanois,
where she held many fêtes, one of which
honoured Franklin.

Howe, Richard, Earl Howe (1726-99),
Vice-Admiral 1775 as Commander-in-Chief
North American station, in cooperation with
his younger brother, General Sir William
Howe. Effected relief of Gibraltar, 1782;
Earldom, 1788.

Hume, David (1711-76), Scottish sceptical philosopher, historian, political economist. Franklin stayed at his home on the occasion of a two-week trip to Scotland in 1771. Hume criticised Franklin's English, but admired his wisdom.

Kames, Henry Home, Lord Kames (1696-1782), Scots judge and author, lord of session as Lord Kames, 1752.

Mecom, born Jane Franklin, Franklin's youngest sister (1712-94), married Edward Mecom (1704-65), a saddler.

Stevenson, Margaret (c. 1706-83), landlady friend, at whose home in Craven Street Franklin stayed through his London years. Her daughter Polly, who married the surgeon William Hewson, became another of Franklin's friends and correspondents, and was with Franklin in Philadelphia when he died.

Whitefield, George (1714-70), strenuous and successful evangelist, joined the Wesley movement while at Oxford and was ordained an Anglican priest in 1739, soon beginning his open-air preaching in England. He made seven journeys to America, founded an orphanage in Georgia, preached up and down the colonies, attracting unprecedented numbers of auditors wherever he went. He was more responsible than any other one man for starting the 'Great Awakening', the first

major religious revival in America.
Conservative in doctrine and belief, he was
radical and emotional in his methods and
aroused bitter antagonism among many of the
clergymen of the chief denominations in both
England and the colonies. Though he was
never able to win Franklin over to his own
religious practices and beliefs, the two
remained warm friends.